HISTORIC MAPS AND VIEWS OF THE OLD SOUTH

The Granger Collection

Black Dog
& Leventhal
Publishers
New York

Published by
Black Dog & Leventhal Publishers, Inc.
151 West 19th Street
New York, NY 10011

Distributed by
Workman Publishing Company
225 Varick Street
New York, NY 10014

MANUFACTURED IN CHINA

ISBN-13: 978-1-57912-919-4

h g f e d c b a

Library of Congress Cataloging-in-Publication Data available on file.

INTRODUCTION
by Donald Dewey

The American South is more than a geographical designation. The region's social, economic, and cultural development has been the horse as often as the wagon of United States history. Historians have often engaged in heated arguments over exactly what the American South encompasses. The textbook definition would embrace the fourteen states below the Mason-Dixon Line and the Ohio River (West Virginia excepted)—Virginia, Maryland, North Carolina, South Carolina, Georgia, Florida, Kentucky, Tennessee, Alabama, Mississippi, Arkansas, Louisiana, Oklahoma, and Texas. Practically speaking, however, the South has become synonymous with the eleven states south of the Potomac River that made up the Confederacy in the Civil War; that is, those on the above list, minus Maryland, Kentucky, and Oklahoma. Within this group are the five states usually referred to as composing the Deep South (Alabama, Georgia, Louisiana, Mississippi, and South Carolina)—the focus of this book.

Natives of the Deep South have never lacked for loyalty. In the words of one resident of the region: "Growing up Southern is a privilege, really. It's more than where you're born, it's an idea and state of mind that seems imparted at birth. It's more than loving fried chicken, sweet tea, football, and country music—it's being hospitable, devoted to front porches, magnolias, moon pies, and Coca-Cola . . . and each other. We don't become Southern—we're born that way."

But even among those not born there, the phrase "antebellum South" prompts an almost conditional response, instantly summoning up images of colonnaded mansions; belles of the ball in long, frilly, tiered dresses; and other trappings of the period between the War of 1812 and the War of Northern Aggression (as the Civil War is often known in the South). Some of these associations are even accurate, despite arising from an era that teemed with all kinds of conflicts, principally those of a racial and economic nature.

The customary depiction of ease, if not outright languor, among the successful in the antebellum South,has tended to mask the importance of aspiration in the region's social relations. For the very rich, this materialized in everything from striving to build the most imposing mansion in the county to wearing the newest fashions copied from European courts. Community etiquette among whites of the upwardly mobile middle classes had more dos and don'ts than Emily Post and Miss Manners combined. The men were bent on being accepted as gentlemen, the women couldn't abide not being viewed as ladies, and offense was taken quickly if someone missed the signals (placing much of the responsibility for the period's description as the "golden age of dueling" on the southern United States). Sipping sweetened tea on the verandah wasn't mere relaxation, it was a proclamation of earned and landed status. The ancient oak on the front lawn reflected tradition and radiated protectiveness, the creek running along the back of the house evoked childhood fantasies of playful innocence, and the gleaming brass knocker on the front door was resorted to only by the rudest of visitors.

Not that conversations over tea on the verandah were freewheeling exercises; on the contrary, whatever the topic was, there was sure to be a cautionary rule lurking and/or a step-by-step prescription for discussing it the right way. Due in part to the social ambitions of Southerners, some seventy books on etiquette were published in the United States in the first half of the nineteenth century—the first such widespread preoccupation with the question of social refinement since the settlement of the New World. For example, it was considered bad manners for women to inquire about the health of their male companions. Men, on the other hand, were counseled never to ask a woman anything, in case a reply veered into disagreeable territory. A gentleman never touched a woman in public, no matter how determined he was to make some point in conversation with her, and she, in turn, had an obligation to pretend that no contact had been made if he slipped up. While it might have seemed courtly in other regions in other ages, the antebellum South cast a disapproving eye on men who sought to help women into their coats or shawls: This was viewed as the next worst thing to touching a woman.

If some of this seems quaint today, it was an integral part of the Deep South identity. Or, as Flannery O'Connor, the Georgia-born author of *Wise Blood* and other prize-winning novels, once put it: "The great advantage of being a Southern writer is that we don't have to go anywhere to look for manners; bad or good, we've got them in abundance."

By the 1870s, the South was changing from a solely agricultural region to an industrial economy. Factories began springing up, defining some Southern cities. Birmingham, Alabama, was a mere footnote before 1879, but in the 1880s, the city mushroomed, powered by iron production. Towns were built around steel production and coal mining as well. In the 1800s, tobacco was no longer just grown in the South; it was processed into cigarettes in Southern plants. Cotton mills were being built in Alabama, Mississippi, and Louisiana. Development of the South's railroad system helped get goods to market. There were only 10,000 miles of track in 1860, but thirty years later railcars were moving along 40,000 miles of track, further propelling the area's industrial push.

Despite industrialization, the region maintained its slow-paced Southern charm. Outside of growing urban areas and burgeoning towns, quiet, picturesque settings abounded. Folks could still fish on the banks of river while enjoying a cool glass of sweet tea.

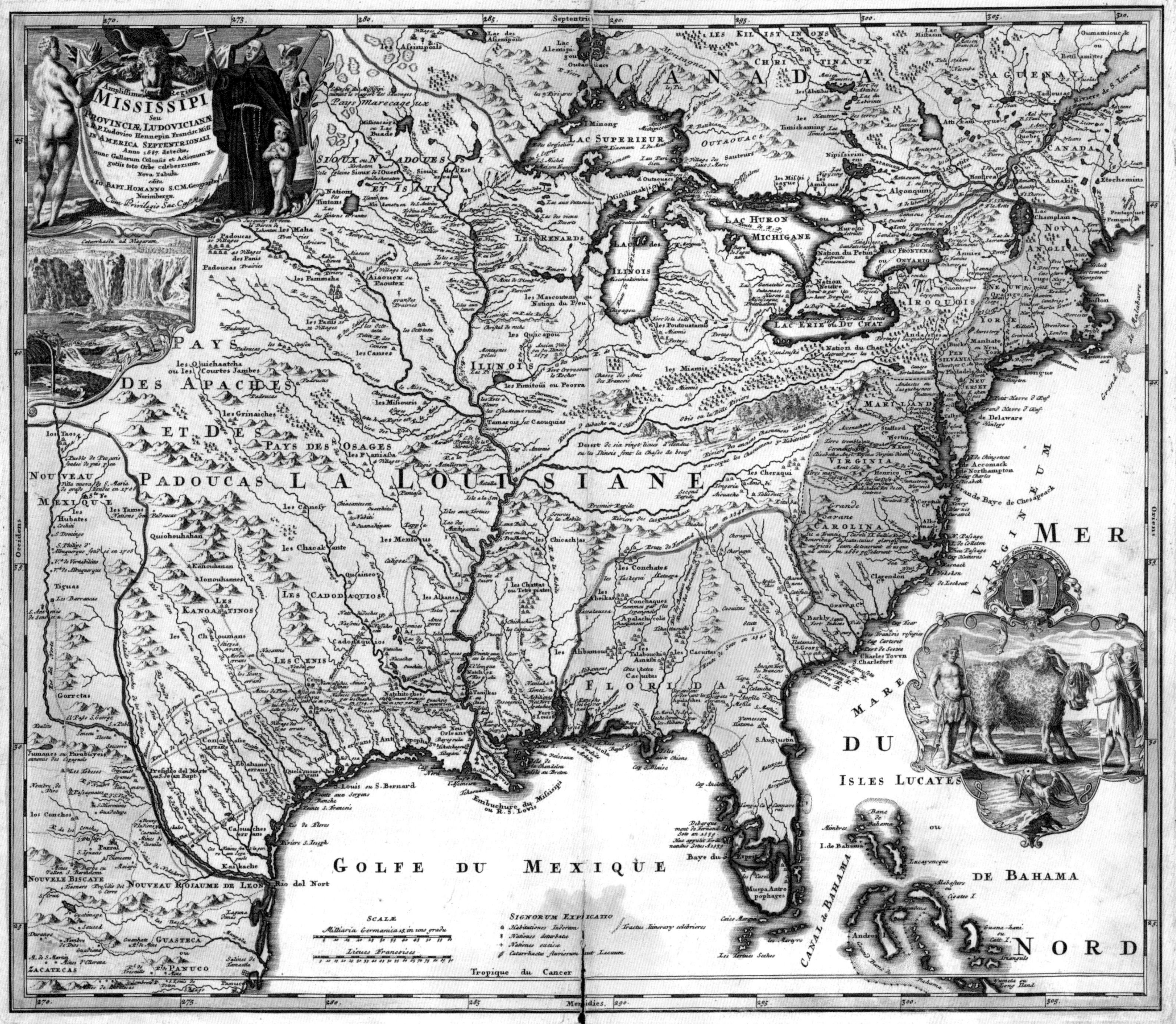

Amplissimæ Regionis
MISSISSIPI
Seu
PROVINCIÆ LUDOVICIANÆ
à R.P. Ludovico Hennepin Francisc Miss
IN AMERICA SEPTENTRIONALI
Anno 1687. detectæ,
nunc Gallorum Coloniis et Actionum Negotiis toto Orbe celeberrimæ,
Nova Tabula
edita
à IO. BAPT. HOMANNO S.C.M. Geographo
Norimbergæ.
Cum Privilegio Sac. Cæs. Maj.
Catarrhacta ad Niagaram
Septentrio
Meridies
Occidens
Oriens
CANADA
LAC SUPERIEUR
LAC HURON
MICHIGANE
LAC des ILINOIS
LAC ERIE ou DU CHAT
LAC FRONTENAC ou ONTARIO
OUTAOUACS
IROQUOIS
NOVA ANGLIA
NOUVEAU MEXIQUE
PAYS DES APACHES ET DES PADOUCAS
LA LOUISIANE
PAYS DES OSAGES
ILINOIS
LES RENARDS
SIOUX ou NADOUESSI ET ISATI
MARILAND
VIRGINIA
CAROLINA
FLORIDA
LES CADODAQUIOS
LES KANOADATINOS
NOUVELE BISCAYE
NOUVEAU ROJAUME DE LEON
GUASTECA
PANUCO
ZACATECAS
Rio del Nort
Embuchure du Missisipi ou R. S. Louis
GOLFE DU MEXIQUE
MER VIRGINEUM
MARE DU NORD
ISLES LUCAYES ou DE BAHAMA
CANAL de BAHAMA
Tropique du Cancer
SCALÆ
Milliaria Germanica 15 in uno gradu
Lieues Françoises
SIGNORUM EXPLICATIO

Amplissima Regionis Mississippi Seu Provinciae Ludovicianae, c. 1720.

Map by Johann Baptist Homann.

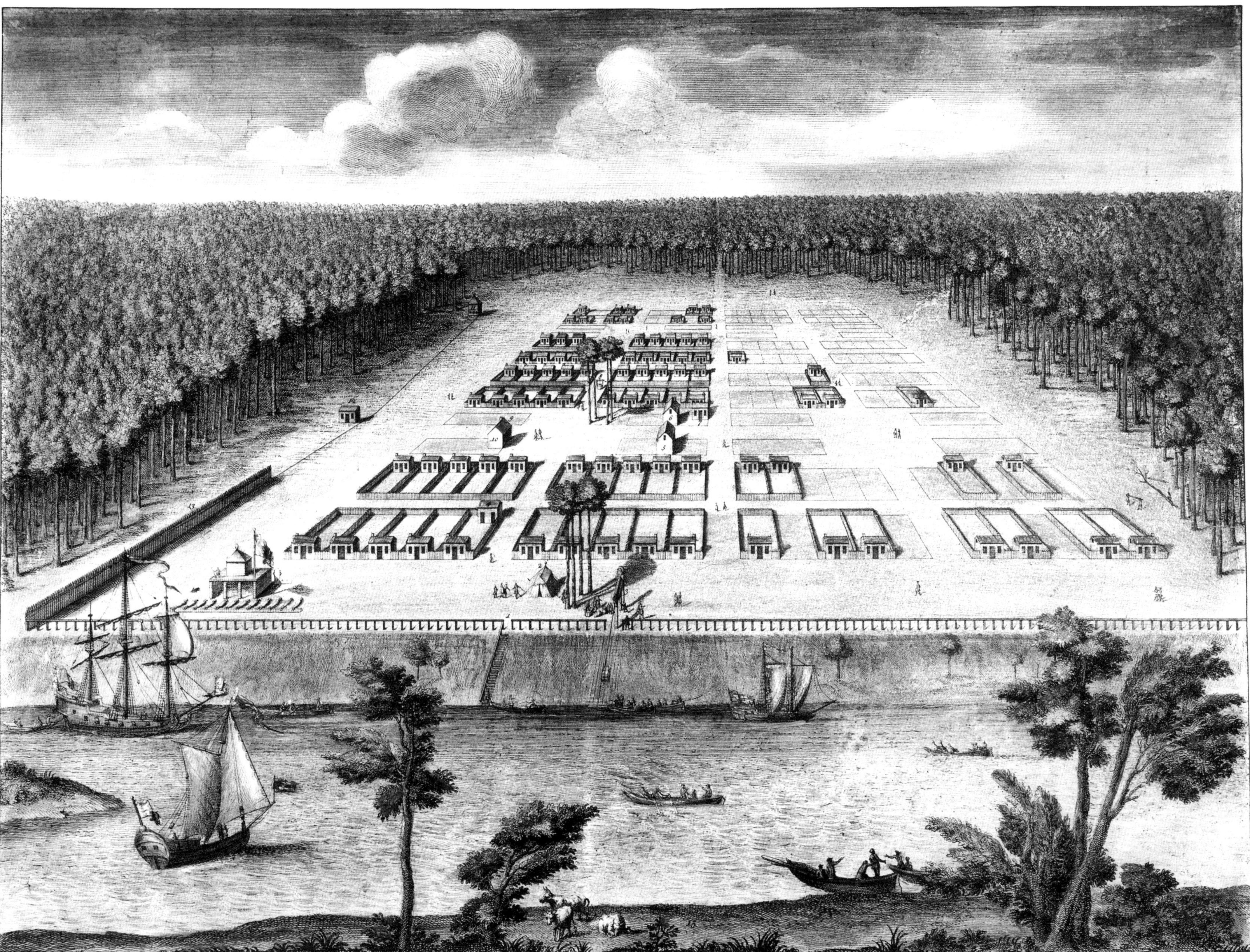

Earliest View of Savannah, 1734.

C. Giroux

Cotton Plantation, c. 1850.

Painting by Charles Giroux.

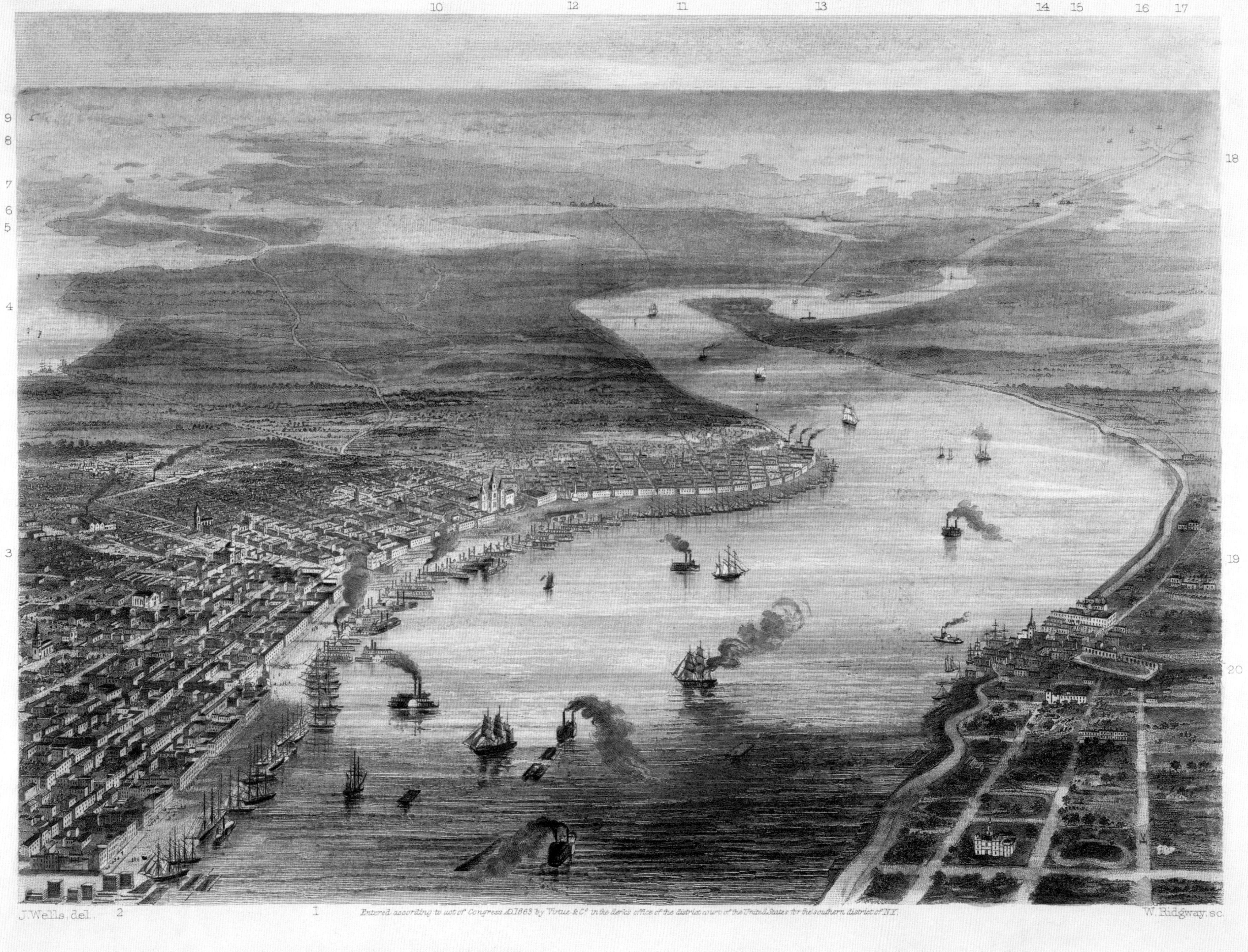

1. Mississippi River.
2. Levee.
3. St Charles Hotel.
4. Lake Pontchartrain.
5. Fort Pike.
6. Rigolets.
7. Lake Borgne.
8. Mississippi Sound.
9. Ship Island.
10. Chandeleur Islands.
11. Gulf of Mexico.
12. Proctorsville.
13. Fort Dupré.
14. Fort St. Philip.
15. Fort Jackson.
16. Balize.
17. South Pass.
18. South West Pass.
19. Mc Donoughville.
20. Algiers.

A Bird's-Eye View of New Orleans, 1863.

VICKSBURG, NATCHEZ AND NEW ORLEANS.
MAIL LINE.
NATCHEZ
ECLIPSE

A Midnight Race on the Mississippi, c. 1850.

Lithograph by Currier & Ives, 1860.

COLTON'S
Rail Road and County
MAP OF THE
SOUTHERN STATES
containing the latest information.
PUBLISHED BY J.H. COLTON, 172 WILLIAM St., NEW YORK.
1864.
KANSAS
IOWA
INDIAN TERRITORY
ARKANSAS
TEXAS
MEXICO
OHIO
KENTUCKY
TENNESSEE
NORTH CAROLINA
SOUTH CAROLINA
GEORGIA
FLORIDA
ATLANTIC OCEAN
Longitude West from Washington
Longitude West from Greenwich
NEW ORLEANS AND DELTA OF THE MISSISSIPPI LOUISIANA
MOBILE HARBOR ALABAMA
ENTRANCE TO PENSACOLA BAY FLORIDA
GALVESTON AND VICINITY TEXAS
VICINITY OF RIO GRANDE
CHARLESTON HARBOR and its approaches S. CAROLINA
JAMES ISLAND
WILMINGTON AND VICINITY N. Carolina
BEAUFORT AND VICINITY N. Carolina
GULF OF MEXICO
GULF STREAM
NEW PROVIDENCE

Colton's Rail Road and County Map of the Southern States, 1864.

Map by Joseph Hutchins Colton.

WAWalker, 1886.

Bombardment of Fort Sumter, 1861.

Painting by William Aiken Walker, 1886.

TOBACCONISTS
ICE
C.R.R.
AWT
W&A
126

Atlanta, Georgia, 1887.

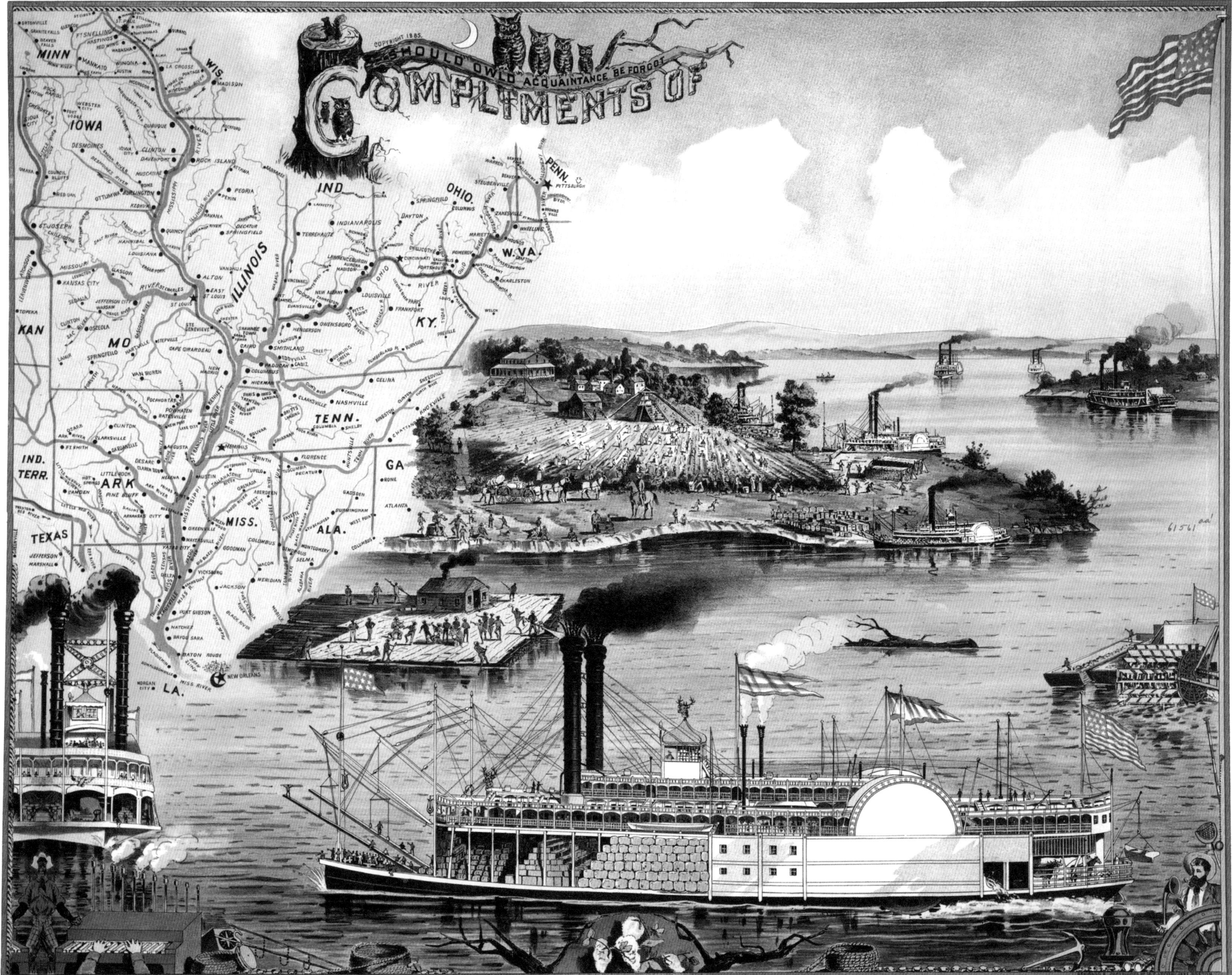
COPYRIGHT 1885.
SHOULD OWLD ACQUAINTANCE BE FORGOT
COMPLIMENTS OF
MINN
WIS.
IOWA
IND.
OHIO.
PENN.
PITTSBURGH
W. VA.
ILLINOIS
KAN
MO
KY.
TENN.
IND. TERR.
ARK
GA
TEXAS
MISS.
ALA.
LA.
NEW ORLEANS

Mississippi Steamboat, 1895.

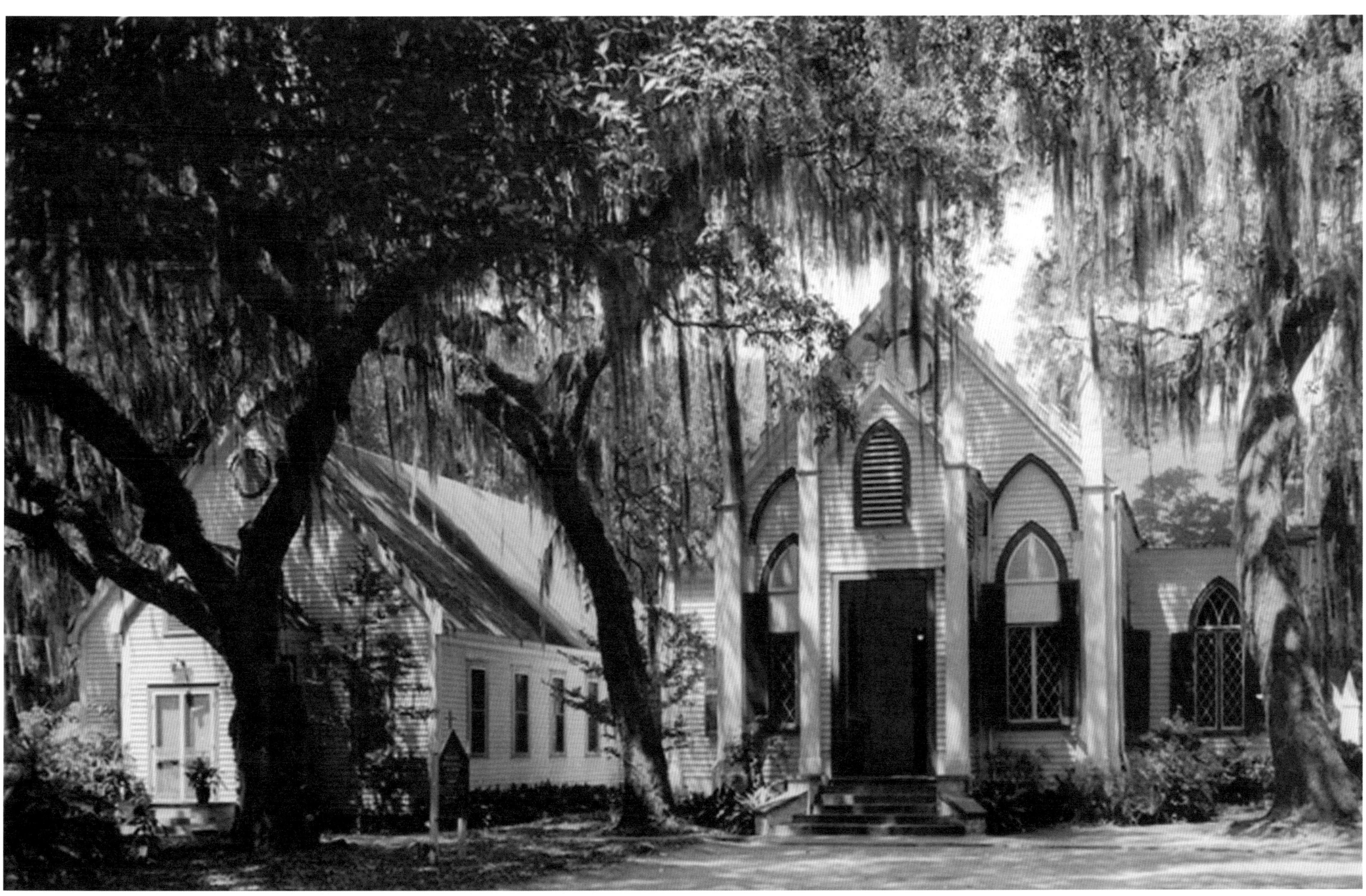

Trinity Episcopal Church in Pass Christian, Mississippi, c. 1900.

Savannah River, c. 1900.

Sinclair Cottage in Ocean Springs, Mississippi, c. 1900.

GRISWOLD & Co
TEXAS
DETROIT PUBLISHING Co

Canal Street, New Orleans, Mardi Gras, c. 1900.

CEMETERY, CHARLESTON
1900, by

South Carolina Oak in Charleston's Magnolia Cemetery, c. 1900.

Forsyth Park, Savannah, c. 1901.

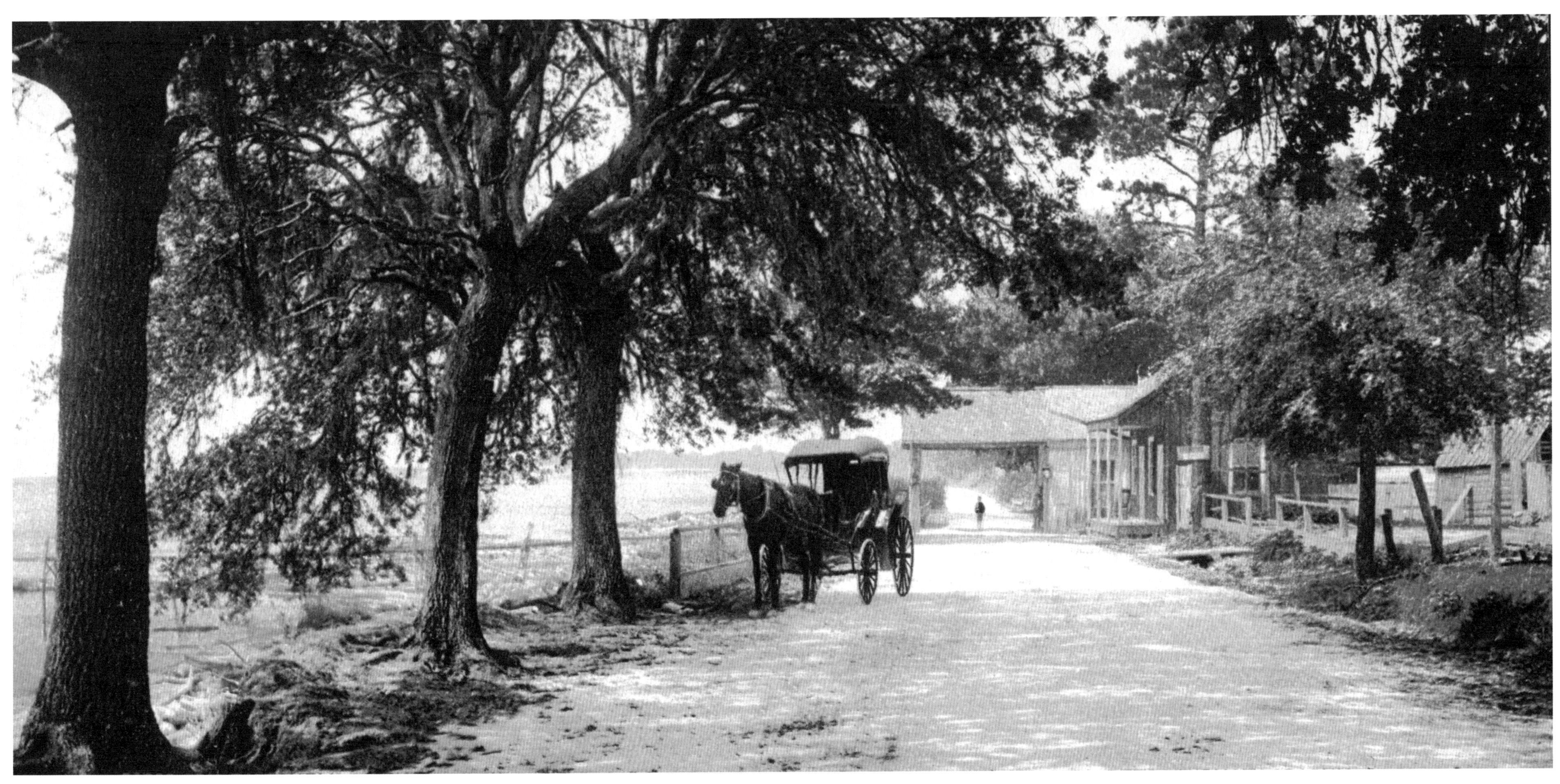

Bay Shell Road, Mobile, Alabama, c. 1901.

Ocean Springs, Mississippi, c. 1901.

Byron N.Y.

Park in the Pines Hotel in Aiken, South Carolina, 1904.

Courtesy of the Museum of the City of New York.

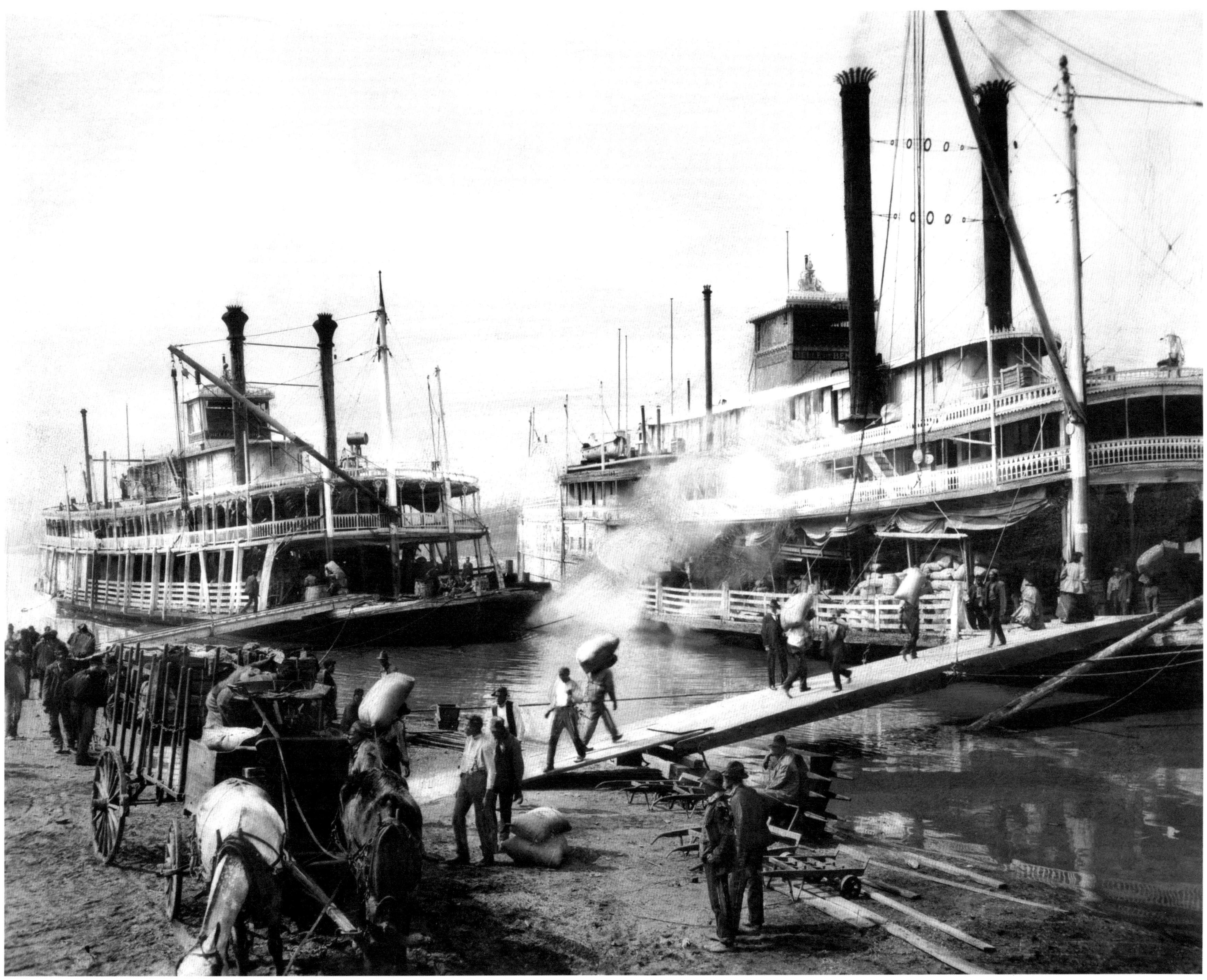

Mississippi Steamboat Landing, 1906.

"THE DAYS OF LONG AGO"
JEFFERSON DAVIS
GEN. ROBERT E. LEE
HALF CENTURY
CONFEDERATE
MEMORIAL
GEN. JOHN B. GORDON
GEN. THOMAS J. (STONEWALL) JACKSON
GEN. G.T. BEAUREGARD
GEN. JOSEPH E. JOHNSTON
GEN. J.E.B. STUART
GEN. ALBERT SIDNEY JOHNSTON
GEN. JOHN B. HOOD
GEN. JAMES LONGSTREET
MAP OF THE
CONFEDERATE STATES
OF AMERICA
FOR
CONFEDERATE WAR SONGS
AND
HISTORICAL DATA
SEE BACK OF THIS CHART
ILLINOIS
KENTUCKY
VIRGINIA
TENNESSEE
ARKANSAS
ALABAMA
GEORGIA
CONFEDERATE MONUMENT UNKNOWN DEAD, ATLANTA, GA.
CONFEDERATE CAPITOL, RICHMOND, VA.
"Who shall break the guards that wait
Before the awful face of Fate?
The tattered standards of the South
Were shriveled at the cannon's mouth
And all her hopes were desolate"
This is to Certify, that
enlisted the day of 186 for years in the
service and was assigned to
and served years months, and days and
was honorably discharged on the day of 186
"Fold up the banners! Smelt the guns!
Love rules. Her gentler purpose runs.
The mighty Mother turns in tears
The pages of her battle years,
Lamenting all her fallen Sons!"

"The Days of Long Ago:" Half-Century Confederate Memorial, c. 1910.

Collage by Fitzhugh Lee.

F.M. POINTER
The Old Reliable
HOUSE MOVER
FISH
&
Honest Weights, Square Dealings
LAKE
FISH
SPECIAL'
TO DAY
RIVER FISH
CAT FISH 20
TROUT
PERCH 15
DRUM 15
BUFFALO 15
EEL 20
SPECIAL'
TO-DAY
RIVER FISH
CAT FISH 20
TROUT
15¢

Fruit and Fish Stand, Birmingham, Alabama, 1936.

Photograph by Walker Evans.

Stanton Hall in Natchez, Mississippi, 1938.

Photograph by Frances Benjamin Johnston.

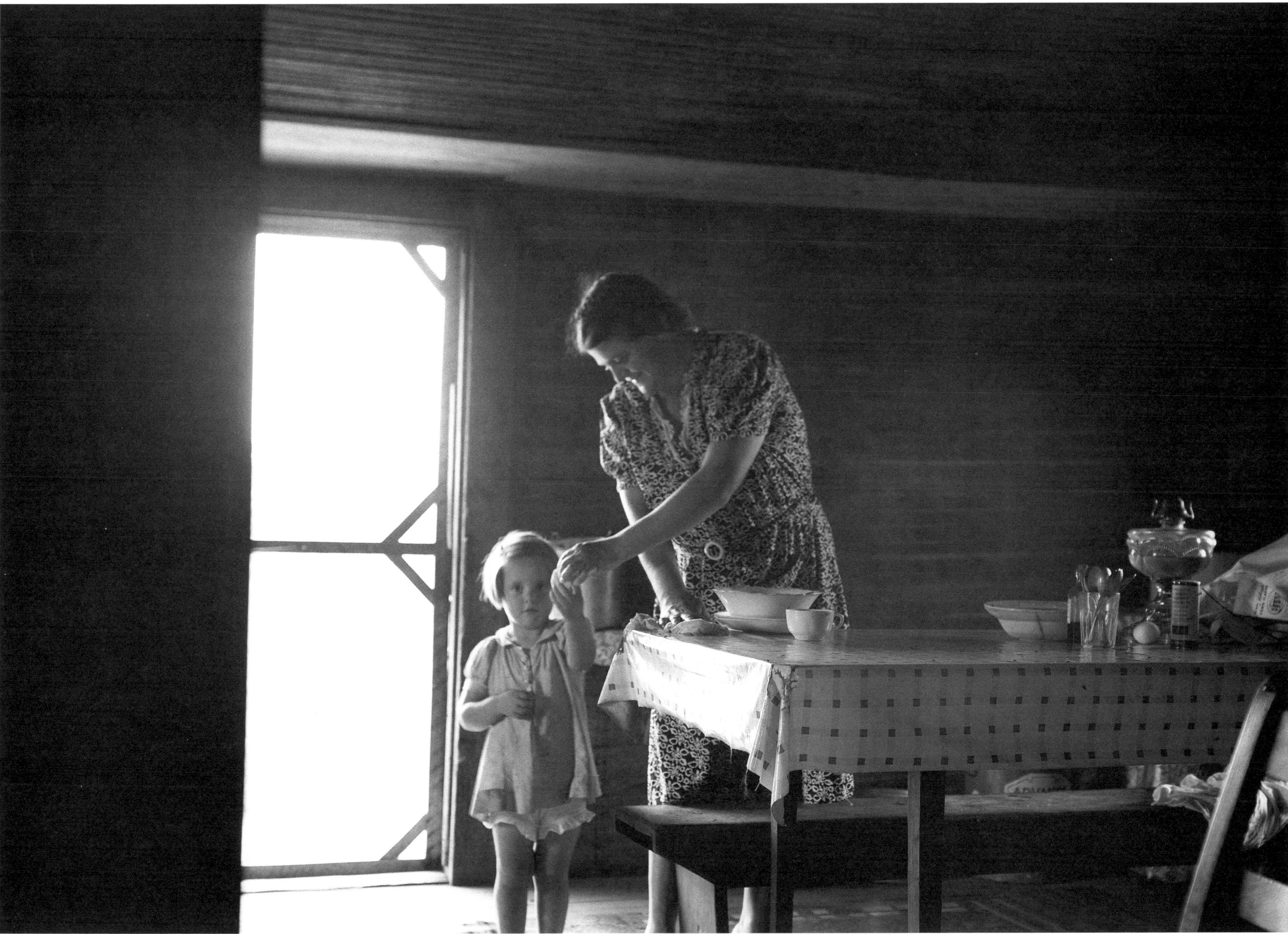

Tobacco Sharecropper, Person County, North Carolina, 1939.

Photograph by Dorothea Lange.

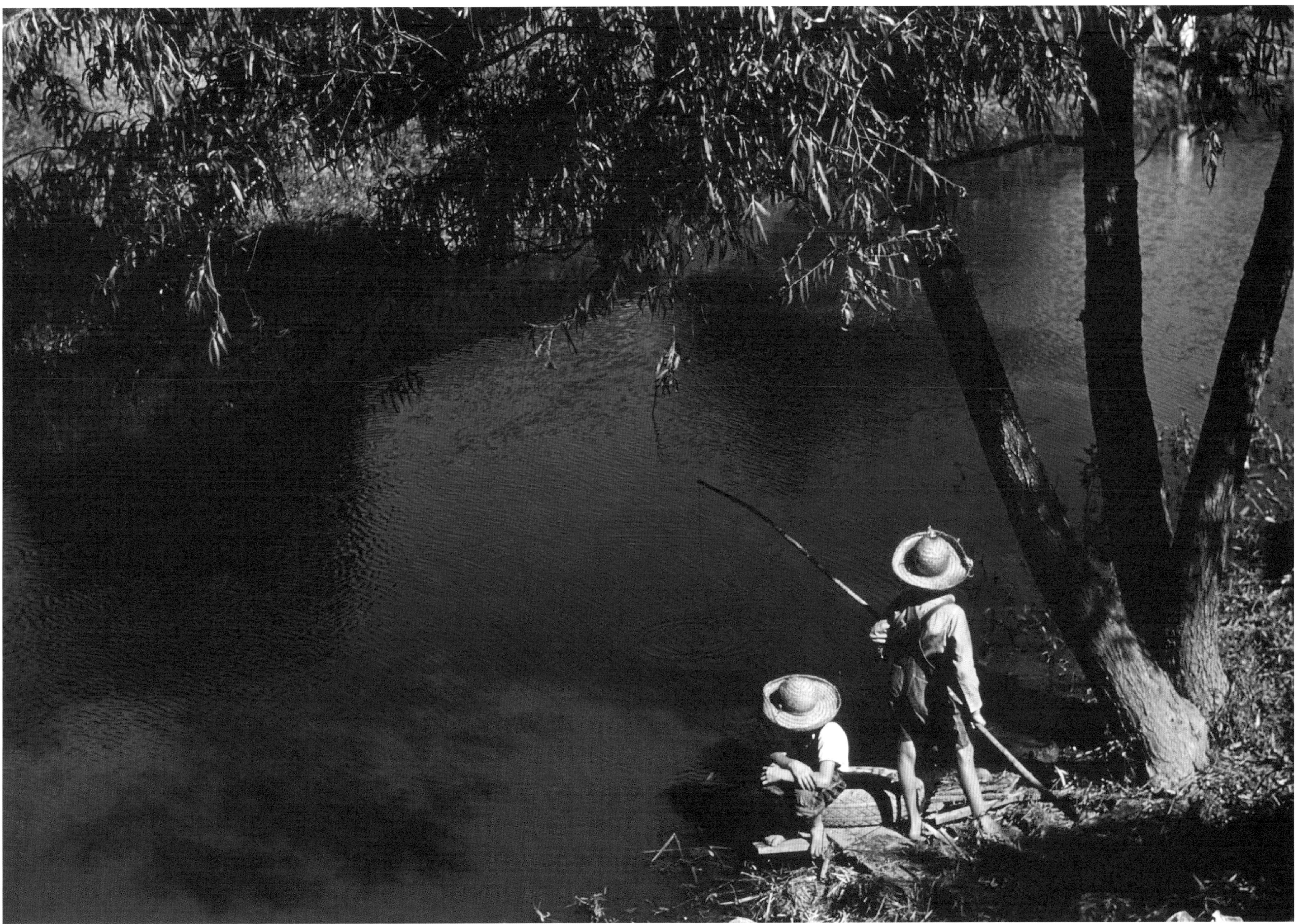

Cajun Boys Bayou Fishing, Schriever, Louisiana, 1940.

Photograph by Marion Post Wolcott.

Amplissima Regionis Mississippi Seu Provinciae Ludovicianae, c. 1720.

Map by Johann Baptist Homann.

One of the earliest renderings of the Mississippi River's course came from the "Amplissima Regionis Mississippi Seu Provinciae Ludovicianae" by Johann Baptist Homann, circa 1720. Unfortunately, it was grossly inaccurate, with the Mississippi and Missouri Rivers (among other things) misplaced. Homann's problem was his chief source of information—the Franciscan missionary Louis Hennepin, a member of a French exploration party thought to have been the first to reach the Mississippi's headwaters in Minnesota. Once back in Paris, the friar turned out a series of writings that blew up his feats to Baron Munchausen proportions. Among his subsequently disproven claims were that he had been the leader of the French exploration mission in Minnesota and that he had been the first to travel the entire length of the Mississippi.

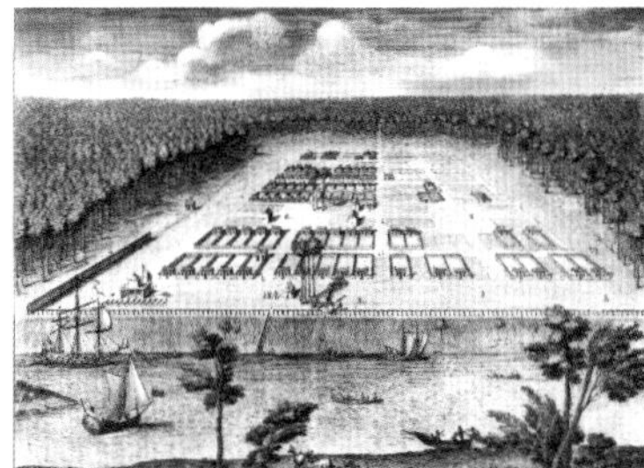

Earliest View of Savannah, 1734.

The previous year, James Oglethorpe, an English general and philanthropist, established Georgia as a debtors' colony, creating a strategic buffer between South Carolina and the Spanish presence in Florida. Savannah owed its early importance to the adjoining Savannah River and quickly developed into a shipping hub.

Cotton Plantation, c. 1850.

Painting by Charles Giroux.

Cotton was first spun in America in John Smith's day in Jamestown, Virginia (1607), but did not serve as the basis for a serious industry until almost two centuries later, thanks to Eli Whitney's cotton gin, invented in 1793. Whitney's invention made for quick separation of the plant's seeds and fibers. The resultant Cotton Belt extended through North Carolina, South Carolina, Georgia, Alabama, Mississippi, western Tennessee, eastern Arkansas, Louisiana, eastern Texas, and southern Oklahoma.

A Bird's-Eye View of New Orleans, 1863.

Before the devastation wrought by Hurricane Katrina in 2005, historians of Louisiana might well have pointed to 1863 as the worst year in the city's history. After decades of flourishing as the Creole-dominated "Queen City of the Mississippi," its import-export trade serving as a model for the rest of the country, New Orleans was invaded by the Union forces of Admiral David Farragut in 1862. By the following year, the occupation under Major General Benjamin Butler was one of the most repressive of the entire Civil War, with the Union officer living up to his nickname of "Beast Butler." He had earned that sobriquet by proclaiming during an earlier assignment that any woman who gave offense to a Union officer was to be regarded as a prostitute, no matter what her actual social station. In New Orleans, he had a minister executed for tearing down a Stars and Stripes, closed all churches that intended, having a Day of Prayer for Confederate soldiers, and shipped out a number of clergymen to New York as potential troublemakers. Only when he began moving against several European consulates as alleged hotbeds of pro-Southern sympathies did Washington rein him in. On the other hand, it was also Butler who, based on earlier experiences in Virginia and the Carolinas, stymied one of New Orleans's regular yellow fever epidemics with an elaborate series of prophylactic measures. Over several decades in the nineteenth century, more than 41,000 people succumbed to the fever in the subtropical climate, including several years in which thousands of victims were recorded. In 1863, only two died.

A Midnight Race on the Mississippi, c. 1850.

Lithograph by Currier & Ives, 1860.

Steamboats were vital to trade, transportation, and communication along the Mississippi for a good part of the nineteenth century. Races were not purely for entertainment either, since they established one vessel's superiority in delivering freight and passengers. The race depicted here apparently took place in the late 1850s between the *Eclipse* and one of a series of boats called the *Natchez*. Overall, there were eight boats named the *Natchez*, followed by a Roman numeral to distinguish one from the other. The first seven met their end through fires, collisions, or the Civil War, while the *Natchez VIII* just ran aground because of the greater speed and economy of the railroads.

Colton's Rail Road and County Map of the Southern States, 1864.

Map by Joseph Hutchins Colton.

From the Confederate point of view, there was little to celebrate about the condition of the railroads during the hostilities. Early in the conflict, the South decided to hoard cotton supplies as an economic incentive to lure England and other foreign nations to join the cause of the secessionists. This, in turn, prompted widespread firings of railroad employees who were no longer needed for customary shipping tasks. Then there was the persistent problem of different track gauges from one state to another, making any ambitious movement of troops on railcars all but impossible. Finally, in the closing phases of the war, the order was given to tear up the tracks from all feeder lines to use the steel for military purposes.

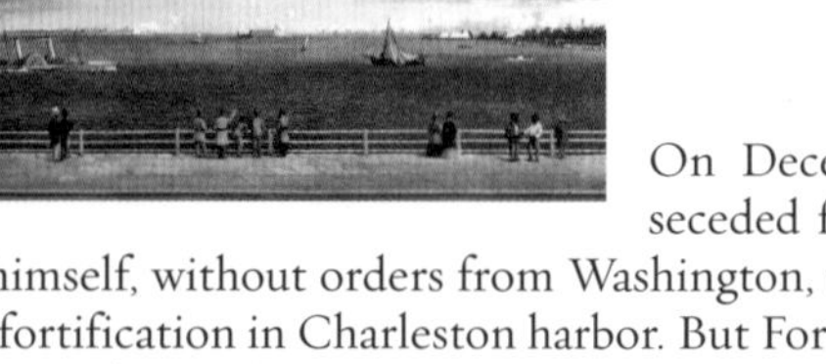

Bombardment of Fort Sumter, 1861.

Painting by William Aiken Walker, 1886.

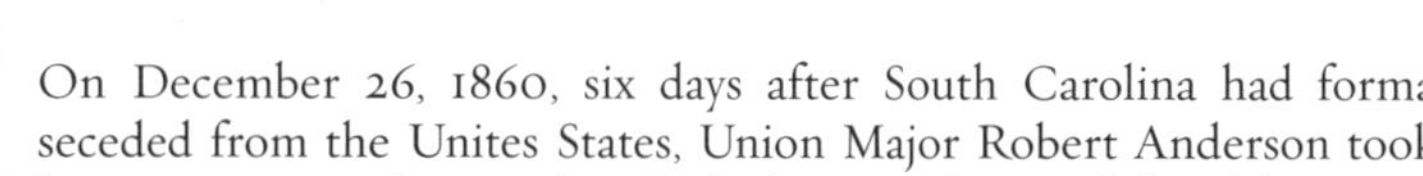

On December 26, 1860, six days after South Carolina had formally seceded from the Unites States, Union Major Robert Anderson took it upon himself, without orders from Washington, to move his one-hundred-plus men from indefensible positions to the fortification in Charleston harbor. But Fort Sumter itself wasn't much of an improvement from a defensive standpoint, having been subject to years of red tape for a construction project that had first gotten under way as far back as 1829. Nevertheless, Anderson refused a Confederate order to surrender in hopes that reinforcements would arrive. That didn't happen. The first shots came from Citadel Academy cadets, turning back a Union relief ship on January 9, 1861. More weeks passed, and it wasn't until April that heavily armed Union ships were sent with food and other supplies. But that proved to be too late for Anderson, who was forced to surrender on April 13. The war had officially begun.

Mississippi Steamboat, 1895.

A color lithograph from the end of the nineteenth century offering a full array of (unintended) Southern caricatures, not the least of which are happy African-Americans floating on rafts, dancing, and playing musical instruments. The map is of the Southern states.

Atlanta, Georgia, 1887.

The city didn't come by its name easily. Its first known non-Indian inhabitant, in 1833, was one Hardy Ivy, who purchased from a middleman what had once been Creek land for $224 and immediately built a log cabin on the property, located at what is today the corner of Courtland and Ellis Streets. The town growing around Ivy over the next couple of years was initially called Terminus for its position at the end of the Western and Atlantic Railroad. When Terminus stopped being a terminus, local politicians sought to rename it Lumpkin in honor of Governor Wilson Lumpkin. Lumpkin himself headed off that dubious choice by proposing instead that it be rechristened Marthasville after his daughter. Martha Lumpkin's entry in the atlas lasted only a couple of years before Atlanta was formally adopted as the city's name in December 1845. There is some debate on the history of origin of the name Atlanta, though some claim it is a variant of Martha Lumpkin's middle name, Atalanta. During the Civil War, Atlanta was the key communications and supply center for the Confederacy and paid for it with the notoriously destructive fire ordered by General William Sherman. Reconstruction was so rapid, however, that it was chosen as Georgia's capital only a year after the end of the war.

Trinity Episcopal Church in Pass Christian, Mississippi, c. 1900.

Built in 1849 in Harrison County along the Gulf of Mexico, the church was pointed to for many years as a prime example of Southern Gothic architecture. That came to an end in August 1969, when Hurricane Camille completely destroyed it. A rebuilt church served parishioners for thirty-six years until, in August 2005, Hurricane Katrina swept it away, along with most of Pass Christian.

Savannah River, c. 1900.

The 301-mile-long river forms most of the border between Georgia and South Carolina. Less clear is the origin of its name, which may or may not have come from a group of Shawnee settled along its banks or from an older Algonquin word for "Southerner." Much of non-Indian Georgian history in the eighteenth and nineteenth centuries coursed along the river, especially around its Savannah and Augusta seaports. Until the channel was closed in 1979, it was possible for barges to make their way from Augusta to the Atlantic Ocean.

Sinclair Cottage in Ocean Springs, Mississippi, c. 1900.

Once owned by Scotsman Duncan Sinclair and a partner, and known as the Sinclair-Faessel Estate, the cottage has long been part of the South's past. In its latest incarnation, since 1973, it has been the site of a condominium complex.

Canal Street, New Orleans, Mardi Gras, c. 1900.

Second only to Rio de Janeiro in the world for its annual pre-Lenten festival, the New Orleans carnival goes on for two weeks, and has done so when not interrupted by wars or natural disasters pretty much every year since being introduced to Louisiana by the French at the turn of the eighteenth century. Just about every day features a colorful parade, for the most part down St. Charles Avenue and Canal Street, during which exotically dressed figures on floats toss beads or other trinkets to the crowds. The culmination of the celebrations comes on the eve of Ash Wednesday and the beginning of Lent, when Mardi Gras (Fat Tuesday) offers a final invitation for indulgence before the Catholic period of remorse and contrition. Some of the traditions associated with the carnival do not have the classical respectability often ascribed to them. For example, the parade figure of Rex the King owes nothing to antiquity, but rather to a coincidental visit during the 1872 carnival by Russian Grand Duke Alexis Alexandrovitch Romanov. Politicians in town were embarrassed that they did not have a royal counterpart to welcome the grand duke properly, so they came up with the genial notion of a comparable fictional local monarch to maintain protocol. The grand duke found it quaintly amusing.

South Carolina Oak in Charleston's Magnolia Cemetery, c. 1900.

The 128-acre graveyard on the banks of the Cooper River was converted from a rice plantation in 1849. It has been the final resting place for numerous local, state, and national politicians.

Forsyth Park, Savannah, c. 1901.

Located in the city's historic district, the thirty-acre park was named after mid-nineteenth-century Georgia Governor John Forsyth. Its most striking feature is a large fountain resembling the Place de la Concorde fountain in Paris. This was no accident, since the mid-nineteenth century saw landscape architects around the United States copying French work, especially public monuments in Paris.

Bay Shell Road, Mobile, Alabama, c. 1901.

Located at the juncture of the Mobile River and Mobile Bay on the Gulf of Mexico, Mobile is Alabama's single seaport. In the middle of the nineteenth century, it trailed only New Orleans in the volume of its cotton exports. For all that, it took a long time for the city to cultivate an Alabama identity. Its first significant role was as the capital of French Louisiana. Then it made its way into the Union as a part of western Florida territories annexed in 1810. After that, it was considered part of the Mississippi Territory. Even when it was finally recognized as belonging to Alabama, it was caught up in the secession movement that led to the Civil War, its seaport serving as a staging area for Confederate soldiers and supplies.

Ocean Springs, Mississippi, c. 1901.

Adjoining Biloxi on the Gulf of Mexico, Ocean Springs is part of an area that has recorded the ever-changing and frequently violent fortunes of land desired by European powers in conflict, leading to a steady succession of international treaties and internal administration changes. There were French periods, Spanish periods, and British periods before Mississippi became a member of the Union in the early nineteenth century. Reflecting the town's long dependence on a tourist economy, spanning everything from spas to gambling, it was named after a popular hotel.

Park in the Pines Hotel in Aiken, South Carolina, 1904.

During the postwar Reconstruction period, entrepreneurs looking for a new way to attract tourist dollars in the Aiken area promoted hotels in heavily wooded locations as aiding health cures. As one brochure put it, they exerted a "soothing and purifying effect upon the mucous membranes of the respiratory passages by the exhalations from pine trees." The first hotel exploiting this approach was the Highland Park. After some years of success, however, the Highland Park demonstrated one of the disadvantages of setting up for business in the woods when, in 1898, a forest fire burned it to the ground. Moreover, its replacement also burned down within a couple of years. Undeterred, the Park in the Pines opened for even bigger business with no fewer than 300 guest rooms. Like the Highland Park, it enjoyed initial success until a fire in 1913 razed it. Unlike the case of the Highland Park, there was no enthusiasm for building another massive inn by borrowing some of the wood from its surroundings.

Mississippi Steamboat Landing, 1906.

To the chagrin of historians, modern ideas of the nineteenth-century steamboat tend toward the vessel depicted in the 1950s Hollywood musical *Show Boat*. (In fact, not even show boats themselves sailed under their own steam, as portrayed in the film.) The true steamboat was usually a three-hundred-ton affair with no fancy trappings that traveled about eight miles an hour, chugging along with passengers and typical cargoes of cotton, tobacco, whiskey, and pork. They were particularly conspicuous up and down the Mississippi during the high waters of late fall and early spring, since this reduced their chances of running aground. Given the scarcity of fixed piers for many years, landings at a plantation or town took place wherever the crew could reach the shore with a stage plank.

"The Days of Long Ago:" Half-Century Confederate Memorial, c. 1910.

Collage by Fitzhugh Lee.

This poster underscores the resolve of many Southerners to remember and even glorify the War of Secession. This map of the secessionist states was executed by Fitzhugh Lee, a nephew of Robert E. Lee and, in his own right, a well-traveled soldier (he took part in both the Civil War and the Spanish-American War), a politician (governor of Virginia between 1886 and 1890), and a diplomat (the representative of two presidents in events prior to the hostilities with Spain). The map is surrounded by the figures of Jefferson Davis, Robert E. Lee, and numerous other Confederate officers. Also depicted are the currency and stamps used by the South and the capitol in Richmond, the capital of the Confederacy.

Fruit and Fish Stand, Birmingham, Alabama, 1936.

Photograph by Walker Evans.

This photograph was taken during the noted trips made to Alabama at the height of the Great Depression by photographer Walker Evans, both for government agencies and for *Fortune* magazine. The trip for *Fortune* was undertaken with writer James Agee, and although the periodical declined to publish the story and photos the pair brought back, they later used their studies of three sharecropping families for the book *Let Us Now Praise Famous Men*. As Evans and Agee recounted it, the owner of the land being worked by the sharecroppers was so hostile to the project that he accused the photographer and writer of being Soviet agents. For their part, members of the families photographed for the book complained that they never even received a copy of *Let Us Now Praise Famous Men*.

Donald Dewey has published 29 books of fiction, nonfiction, and drama, as well as scores of stories and articles for magazines and other periodicals. As a writer and editor, he has specialized in city profiles, both pertaining to the United States and abroad. Some of his writings have been incorporated into college history texts. Among his books are the history of American political cartoons (*The Art of Ill Will*) and the history of baseball fans (*The Tenth Man*).

Stanton Hall in Natchez, Mississippi, 1938.

Photograph by Frances Benjamin Johnston.

The owner of some sixteen-thousand acres of cotton fields, Frederick Stanton oversaw the construction of his ornate home between 1851 and 1857, buying an entire city block to accommodate it. The mansion's features—everything from Corinthian columns and bronze chandeliers to marble fireplaces and wrought-iron frames—were shipped in from France, Italy, and other European countries. As it turned out, just about everybody except Stanton got to enjoy the mansion because he died a month after its completion. For some years it was used as a college for young girls, then fell into disrepair before being taken over by the Pilgrimage Garden Club, which has made it one of the premier tourist attractions in Natchez. The Hall was declared a national historic landmark in 1974. First-time visitors regularly comment that it seems familiar to them, suggesting that they previously visited Disneyland's Haunted Mansion, all but copied from the Mississippi structure. The photo of the mansion was taken by Frances Benjamin Johnston, one of the first women photojournalists in the United States and the official White House photographer for five presidents.

Tobacco Sharecropper, Person County, North Carolina, 1939.

Photograph by Dorothea Lange.

Long practiced in several European and Asian countries, sharecropping was the most widespread economic solution to the devastation left in the wake of the Civil War in the South. The standard sharecropping agreement called for poor whites or blacks to work land for 50 percent of what they grew. The landowners pocketed not only the other 50 percent but also usually managed to shave off payouts by selling seed and supplying other agricultural tools to the laborers. Variations on this kind of agreement might simply charge rent for the land, with the sharecropper keeping everything he produced or, alternatively, the sharecropper being paid as an employee but keeping none of the crops. The system remained the backbone of the South's economy well into the 1930s and contributed mightily to the antagonistic racial attitudes still in place—emancipation or no emancipation. During the Depression, government figures estimated that there were 5.5 million whites and 3 million blacks working as sharecroppers in the Southern states. What finally undermined the system was mechanization and the subsequent migration of African-Americans, in particular, to Northern cities.

Cajun Boys Bayou Fishing, Schriever, Louisiana, 1940.

Photograph by Marion Post Wolcott.

The Cajuns followed a twisted, and sometimes tortuous, trail to end up in the state. Their ancestors were members of a French-speaking Canadian area called Acadia, this in itself a linguistic corruption of what explorer Giovanni da Verrazzano in the fifteenth century compared to Arcadia ("place of refuge") in ancient Greece. After losing their *r*, most Acadians also lost their homeland in the region around Nova Scotia and the Canadian Maritimes because of the British victory in the French and Indian War (1754–1763). The so-called Great Expulsion that followed saw thousands of Acadians either gaining passage to France or setting out across America, with an appreciable number ending up in what is today's Terrebonne Parish in Louisiana. For many years, the Cajuns were treated as third-class citizens. Organized government campaigns were launched to wipe out their archaic language, which, after a couple of centuries, had become as impenetrable to mainstream French speakers as to those with English as a mother tongue. It was only in 1980 that Cajuns were recognized as a distinct ethnic group in their own right.

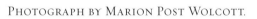